I0088203

Oblige the Light

Oblige the Light

Danuta E. Kosk-Kosicka

Winner of the Harriss Poetry Prize
Michael Salcman, Prize Series Editor
and 2014 Contest Judge

CITYLIT
PRESS
Baltimore, Maryland

© 2015, Danuta E. Kosk-Kosicka

Library of Congress Control Number: 2015937032
ISBN 978-1-936328-20-8
CityLit Project is a 501(c)(3) Nonprofit Organization
Federal Tax ID Number: 20-0639118
All rights reserved. No part of this book may be
reproduced or transmitted in any form or by any means,
electronic or mechanical, including photocopy, recording,
or any information storage and retrieval system,
without prior permission from the publisher
(except by reviewers who may quote brief passages).
Printed in the United States of America
First Edition

Book Design: Gregg Wilhelm
Cover Art: Photography and collage by Danuta E. Kosk-Kosicka
Author Photograph: Andrzej J. Kosicki

CITYLIT
PRESS

c/o CityLit Project
120 S. Curley Street
Baltimore, MD 21224
410.274.5691
www.CityLitProject.org
info@citylitproject.org

for Piotruś

Contents

Introduction

When you open *Oblige the Light* by Danuta E. Kosk-Kosicka, you will enter a magical space in which trees have "mitten-shaped leaves" and "grenade-like mulberries," a river "flows through us to the Milky Way," and "the clouds weigh down on the massive ridges pinned by lightning cracks." Astonishing metaphors and precise description of natural forces and historical events results in an atmospheric Magical Realism that borders on the Surrealistic. The strangeness is further torqued by the not-quite idiomatic syntax and language employed. Evidently English is not the native language of the voice in the poems even though almost all were written in English. Then, too, there is an emotional reserve that is almost gnomic so that life's most important subjects—the death of a parent, political oppression, one's aesthetic response to art and nature—can be discussed without forced sentimentality. The poems are the work of a profoundly serious temperament and a professional translator of world into word. In order to understand why the poems are here it helps to know something about their order and how the poet came to be here.

Danuta E. Kosk-Kosicka, this year's winner of the Harriss Poetry Prize, was born in 1949 in Lublin, the ninth-largest city in Poland, approximately one hundred miles south-east of Warsaw, close to the Soviet Union border. Lublin had been a center of Jewish life in Europe until the community and its famous yeshiva were destroyed in the Holocaust. Danuta spent her entire childhood living under another oppressive dictatorial system in which every aspect of life was under state control, even so-called political demonstrations and sporting events. Moments of freedom and happiness were relegated to quiet times and dark corners when and where jokes against the communist regime might be uttered. From the first she was steeped in poetry. Like other Polish children, she grew up studying the great Romantic poets of Poland such as Adam Mickiewicz; furthermore, her own mother was a well-published poet whose work Danuta has been translating into English. Eventually, Danuta earned a Ph.D. in biochemistry and a postdoctoral fellowship from the Muscular Dystrophy Association for two years of study in San Francisco. She left Poland in June just before the Solidarity movement broke out with shipyard strikes in August of 1980, the very year Czesław Miłosz (1911-2004) won the Nobel Prize in Literature. Danuta has lived in Baltimore since 1981, following her professor's academic move from California to the University of Maryland. Martial law was declared in Poland on December 31st of that year and after the birth of her son in 1983, Danuta and her husband decided to remain in America. She felt that the prospects for raising a child in her homeland were rather bleak. Her subsequent research career at Johns Hopkins (1991-1996) was cut short by a chronic illness. Danuta had written some poetry in Polish during her youth, but in 1996, coincidentally the year that Wisława Szymborska (1923-2012), a protégé of Miłosz, also won the Nobel Prize, Danuta not only gave her poetry serious intellectual attention but wrote it in English. It was about this time that important American poets like Charles Simic and Robert Hass, both past poets laureate of the United States, were introducing Americans to contemporary poetry from central and eastern Europe. Because of the isolation and dislocation of cultural life under communism, older literary movements like Surrealism remained important. Something like the terseness and strangeness of Simic's work can be detected in Danuta's poetry.

However, Danuta's most direct artistic connections are to other women poets. It is no accident that she has translated poems by her mother, Lidia Kosk, and Szymborska from Polish into English, and has published in Poland her translations from the English of three former Maryland poets laureate: Josephine Jacobson, Lucille Clifton, and Linda Pastan. Equally, the constant shuttling back and forth between the two languages must have had an impact on her work. The poems in *Oblige the Light* cover almost the entire period of her serious engagement with the art form, from 1997 to 2011. The epigraphic, Imagist quality of many of the poems, such as "Girl in the Red Coat," remind me of H.D. (Hilda Doolittle), the feminist member of Ezra Pound's circle. The strong visual sense in her work is underlined by her love of modernist paintings and motion pictures. She admits (under great pressure) that some of her favorite painters are Surrealists like Magritte and Miró and mentions Gabriel Garcia Marquez on the short list of her favorite writers. But in general Danuta rejects any of them as "models"; remarkably, she is a self-taught poet who is now a co-editor of one of our leading regional literary magazines.

In selecting Danuta E. Kosk-Kosicka as the winner of this year's Harriss Poetry Prize I admit to no sense of impartiality. She is that self-taught late-comer that one must pay attention to. She is that central European voice that wobbles between the all-too-real and the fantastic. When she writes "I see trampled bread on the empty road," you have to believe her. When she describes her father's wound in its "roundness and depth, /stuffed with his handkerchief, /the sinking, the droning, the swarming/ of flies," you have to bend to her power. Whether free form, sonnet, or prose poem, there is an intensity that goads your conscience. She is the real thing.

Michael Salcman
Series Editor and 2014 Judge
Harriss Poetry Prize

while trying to peel off
bluish-grey shadows
from the sparkling snow
I rescue a pale-blue *imagine*

Baltimore, 2013

The Thin Blue Line between Still and Alive

In the Art Gallery students create moving paintings.
They stand or sit by their chosen portrait on the wall—
same pose, same splendid costume,
here a blue sash, a sword, there a yellow rose.

At the strike of one they stir, casually walk away,
leaving the background and the still selves.

I come alive on the background of a jet plane
pierced with a row of doors. The farthest opens
on a sandy Mazovian plain with Chopin's weeping willow.

My hand reaches through the door, brings out
a clover leaf, lilac flower, grain of sand,
a walnut from the tree guarding the whitewashed house.

I glance ahead. And back again. Step by step, I move on.

My Mother at Twelve
Minkowice, Poland, 1940

Hours of waiting at the bakery,
all my money for a last loaf of bread.
Now, cycling kilometers to hunger at home.

Near the hamlet where roads cross,
I see German soldiers rounding up people,
my friend Hana among them.

I jump off the bicycle, run toward Hana
with the still-warm bread. "Death for helping Jews,"
the soldier points his gun at my chest. I trip and fall;
a bullet wails.

When darkness lifts,
I see trampled bread on the empty road.

The Movie in My Head
Eastern Europe after V-E Day

I see the sun, fields,
ramshackle hut of a country station,
and sitting, his back to the wall,
a young soldier in olive-green uniform,
puffing on a cigarette.

I hear the rustle
of ripening June wheat,
bees in the clover
and the footsteps.

I see him entrapped
by a band of men
secretly drawing guns.

I hear the alarm of approaching train,
the swelling sounds: the tumble of words,
struggle, running, thumping of shots
and his leap—

       the hut, the sun, the fields
       distant now;
       up close
       coarse wooden boards of the freight car,
       scattered straw

       the wetness, the stickiness,
       wound's roundness and depth
       stuffed with his handkerchief,

the sinking, the droning, the swarming
of flies.

When the train arrives at the junction
Military Red Cross finds him—
they carry out the soldier on a stretcher.
His trophy a fistful of straw. If he pulls out
the lucky straw, he will be my father.

May Day
Warsaw, 1965

The teachers checked off our names, assigned each of us
long sticks with placards, banners, red crepe poppies
or cerulean cornflowers. One hour into practicing the waving
& chanting my friend & I snuck our banner

over to a latecomer. Stepping back
one row at a time, chased by the loudspeakers
in the flutter of white-and-red flags,
we hurried to Krakowskie Street
& ran to the Blikle Patisserie.

The line moved slowly behind the glass door.
"Ten of them, please." A silver tong
transferred the sugar-glaze roundness one by one
onto a white cardboard square. Arranged in two rows,
wrapped with crisp paper, secured with a yellow string,
a gold-lettered *Blikle* seal, they belonged to us.

Freed of all money we walked for one hour
to our neighborhood park where on a bench
we set them between us: unstrung, unwrapped,
specks of orange peel glistening in the glaze,
scent of rose marmalade in their heart.
We bit in, one by one.

Now we should be marching, now nearing
the stands, now waving at our leaders, now chanting:
Long Live Comrade Wiesław!
Long Live the Friendship With the USSR!
At the third doughnut we had to stop.

Long Live Proletarian Internationalism!
We were nauseous.
Long Live the Immortal
Revolutionary Doctrine, Marxism-Leninism!

Then all the schools had passed the stands,
the chanting, the banners, the crepe flowers
were stowed away till the next parade.

Queuing for Lenin

Cooing. Pigeons. Moscow hotel. The dream. I am waking up in my green room to the cooing of doves in the crabapple tree and the scent of hot cocoa topped with froth of egg whites. Sunday breakfast treat of my Polish childhood. It's the day of the giant whale. The whale, talk of the land-locked town. Blue circus tent, people pushing alongside something huge, dark. Perched on my father's shoulders, I am a blue-eyed, flaxen-haired question mark: where is the whale, where are its eyes, is it alive?... Dressed up, I get on the subway. On Red Square the queue is endless. After days on trains from all over the Soviet Union, the citizens wait and wait. A foreigner, I make it to the short foreigners' queue. Inside, people progress at a constant pace in the silence of granite chambers. Blue sparkles in the black stone vaults. Shivers of anticipation. Guards with weapons. Measured pace, no slowing down, no whispers, hands down at your sides. There he is. The column of people walks around the three sides of the glass case in respectful awe. He is small in the yellow light. Dressed in a dark suit, white shirt, a tie. Eyes closed. No stopping, moving on, moving on. Out on the square I face the crowds waiting under a huge red banner: Lenin forever alive.

Sunday Like No Other
Baltimore, 1981

Third floor, left, first door. He opens, smiling wide.
She is early. His suitcases line the wall.
He hasn't heard; he doesn't know. She steps over the threshold.
"You can't go home, this morning the general in his dark
shades declared martial law."
His green eyes, his impeccable manners from Old Europe.
"But Sarah, you will take me to the airport, right?"

Her car radio repeats the world news, "Martial law in Poland.
No travel allowed. Phones disconnected. Tanks in the streets.
Solidarność banned. Curfew at 20:00."

At the airport he presents his return ticket to Warsaw.
His will be the last flight.
"Don't go into that darkness," she repeats in her head.

The call for boarding. His green eyes.
Head high, he walks toward the exit.
Her arm lifts and waves. The door shuts.

At the Seaside Café

Smell of fried fish, packed parking, swinging doors,
crunchy peanut shells scattered on the floor,
license plates on the walls. General
Zapata, Coca-Cola girl. Beer, cold.
Outside low windows, slow-swaying tall grass.
Inside, the waiters at low tide: long wait
for our main course. Clatter, laughter, thick air.
Ceiling fan splits and reassembles waves.
Entangled in noise, music plays somewhere.
From his small bowl, our son feeds boiled peanuts
to the fish on his beach shirt, dozes off.
We fish from our big bowl, crack the shells, catch
bits of notes, fragments of the familiar
seeping through the maze. We make out the song.

Paintings in a Gray-Walled Waiting Room
after Chagall

A village. Houses upside down. A green cow,
pink air. Onion-domed church, a synagogue.
A groom, a bride, a long white dress.
They float, they dance. A fiddler.
A blue goat playing a violin.

In the village where I live houses are shades of beige.
Beige-brown deer devour colors. No couples dance
above the steepled church. In the sky sometimes
a heron flies, mostly hawks and planes.
A groom and his bride, at a crab feast, wear blue jeans.

A goat and a cow graze behind the picket fence
when I drive to school with my son.
The cello is still bigger than him. Tonight
I watch my son's eyes smile, embracing his cello.
He floats. Bouquets. Bach concerto.

Fabled Roosters of Kazimierz

Once I went to the town where pretzels grew
rooster-shaped. Lines of buyers formed at dawn.
Aromas from the bakery weaved through
garden, castle hill, tiny crooked streets.
From the attic room where I slept forty
years ago the young sun still guides me down
the murmuring stairs on a dew-beaded
path through the garden of scents. I pull
feathery greens from shimmering rows—
onions, carrots, red beets. The soil inhales
my contented toil, exhales the hoed weeds.
Iridescent roosters peck at unlocked earth.
In the expanding summer the good witch
grants me memories and multihued dreams.

Lucky Shows Up Seventy Years Later

Poland, February 2002

Ah, Lucky—good dog, good doggie.
You have been away for so many years
you wag your warped tail, stretch,
you want me to follow.

Where are we going?

Ah, towards the river across the field
unfurled like a whitened cloth.
The dew has fallen. Seems
the cows are back in their sheds.
It's quiet.
I can still smell the milk
and the dust stirred by chains,
dragged on their way from the meadows.

We are coming to the bridge
of pine planks my father
nailed together—but it is gone.

Lucky, you are feathery white
like the chicken you snatched
when I was a teenage boy in the village
which is no more on the river
that now flows through us to the Milky Way.

Next Time

Where will I find you when I come
Wings parting clouds, feet steadying
On the ground

What will I see in your yellow room,
Where you no more watch
The forest clearing on the wall

How will it feel to touch your name
On the green-veined stone
With my reflection in a candle flame,

With the sky wide open, trees out of leaves
Will we walk again as we did—
My cold hand in your warm hand?

Visitation

That pull. To the place
enclosed by a sandstone box.
From all over I am, again.

They begin to peel off
the rotting and dried leaves
with a brush scraping every crevice.
From a jug they pour water,
it seeps into pores.
They wash the stone
inch by inch, head to toe,
all four sides
and dry with a towel.
When they get to the lettering I begin tingling.

Then they bring out
the pots with lavender flowers.
And candles.
        Were I alive like them
I would kneel.
And fall into silence.

They stare into flames.
A yellow birch leaf drifts in.

Darkness of Her Head

after Gauguin

On the pillow of light
lies the darkness of her head.
Encased in Prussian blue fear,
the abundance of her golden flesh stifled
under layers of green-brown.
Alone like this at the mercy of *Tupapaus.*

Move.
Abandon the dark layers.
Move away from that one.
Start a new painting.

Paint the mountain in its vibrato ocher,
the ocean in broad ultramarine,
mango pears in short strokes
on the ground, in the bowl,
mango flowers in the long sweeps of hair.

Move.
Like the orchid bloom furled
in the green womb, sensing its way.
Oblige the light

till you can feel the spray on the wave
crest, the strength of the red
mountain, the scent of mango.
Till the stillness feels right.

A Gatherer

The tip breaks off when I pull down the loaded branch.
On tiptoes, I reach again, as far as the tree allows
through its mitten-shaped leaves. I gently touch
purple-black, grenade-like mulberries.

Plump, elongated. They bleed onto my palms.
My forebears—with their hands, flint knives,
sickles, wicker baskets, clay pots—gathered
what the forest and meadows bore and shared.

Bow and arrows aside, leashed to a plough, they
opened the earth wider for their barefoot heirs.
A field yields tree stumps, stones, domesticated crops,
bullet-pierced helmets, grenades unexploded

during the great war. A mastodon rib with a bone shard,
a spear point driven home by an ice-age hunter—
gathered at the break of the 21st century.
My stained hands reach for more.

Girl in the Red Coat

The phone rings.
I like red phones. I answer.
I am wearing a red coat.
I am the little girl in my family album.
I am the little girl in the movie.
No, I am almighty.
I say:
I will send you help right away.
Do not get on the train.
Do not go through the gate.
Do not enter the chamber.

In the Background the Waltz from *Doctor Zhivago*

In a movie a train
Like a toy—in whose hands?—
   Runs on a white plain, sways,
Jerks on the tracks
   Pursued by a plumed snake.

Where, where, where
   A land rolled out for play—
Who, who, who

The ones who packed themselves
Fifty to a freight car with a choking stove
   May have had enough force
To thrust through the thick pane
Of the dry frozen universe
   And see yellow flowers above
   The blades of grass.

The unlucky ones in the strangling
Arms of the army with red stars
   Had no chance—forced into freight cars
Thrown in the hollows
In the Katyń forest.
Clots on their bulleted heads,
Tied hands, blindfolded words
Thaw in the spring.

        To freeze again
Over and over
        To not forget.

Where, where, where, who, who, who
            Scatters dead flowers, turns
Earth into a crippled toy planet

The Voices

are muffled
by the walls. Someone
is spelling: P-r-i-z-r-e-n
or M-e-j-a.

Or is it C-o-l-u-m-b-i-n-e,
the name of the fragile
plant outside my door,
with blooms like bleeding

bells with five spikes? Is it
a spelling bee, a lesson
in biology or social studies?
Mountains lie in snow.

They are singing do-re-mi-fa-so-
the mountains, the children,
or the sudden swarm
of bullets? A row of metal

lockers swallows them
and then, swaying, kneeling,
curling up, the row hits the ground.
A river flows by, but the limp bodies

stay frozen, only one man's
hand in spasm lifts up.
Will the old Charon ferry
them one by one, taking lead

as the 20th-century coin?
Over the deep abyss
where the hearts sank
the banging on the doors

and the crystal sound
of smashed glass
clot into notes, do-re-mi-fa.
But the music sheets are empty,

the lines are treading to refugee
camps, the notes can't stay,
shaped into bullets.
A woman with dried eyes

listens to the silence bundled
in her arms. A young man
pulled away spells: h-e-l-

Echocardiogram

I watched my heart beat, pump blood on the screen.
My blood was blue, my blood was red.
The surges were coming strikingly fast.
Spilled lightning storms through the valves that open
and close. The mitral valve, an untamed
galloping horse. The aortic, swishing
like a ghost train. Next I heard the tricuspid,
a gulping frog. Waves, spikes, walls, gates. Dangers
lurking in sounds, embedded in red.
And I thought of the Red River rising
above its flood stage, up to twenty-six
fire-tinted feet. I saw gutted buildings.
Over for now, news and my test. Echo
of valves and fires in red rivers stays.

This Is Not My Stomach
after Margritte

A giant green apple of pain. Paper,
pen, displaced by computer screen. A hand,
no connection. Inside, under the skin,
the muscles and rib cage, the J-shaped
stomach sac. The hand moves in; scorched by
low pH, click-clicks its way up the e-
sophagus, startles the vomiting reflex,
slips off the tongue to the paper, transforms
into an ink blot, pressing the mouse
to spell: p-o-o-r s-t-o-m-a-c-h. A quick click
on the breathing chest draws out pain from
the pylorus on the computer screen.
On the desk paper and pen slowly crawl
to reclaim connection with the hand.

An Artist Paints the Event

Where is the second turtle?
Concerned that time is running out,
she counts the animals. The line
is casual, straying to the sides.

Black rhino flanking a gray elephant,
only one hare, no rooster in sight.
Why aren't they prepared, paired up?
The clouds weigh down on the massive ridges

pinned by lightning cracks
in the blackened sky.
At least there is no violence
in the crowd. The cow, udder-full,

looks past the muted lion to the moose
away from the vessel and the passageway.
The water is dark.
Highlights fall on a blur of doves

and two swans painted in the cove.
Are they boarding or leaving the Ark?

The Sun Comes Out in San Luis Potosí

The wind weakened to a murmur, a rose
unpretentious in her morning pink, sheets
of pure blue Mexican sky and against
it, ready to unzip and burst, palm leaf—
not fulfilled yet, out only three inches
wriggling in the breeze when I leave for church.
Indian summer in the *churrigueresque*
gold chapel: under Madonna's soft gaze,
mother's face above her infant boy, their
hair dark like *Señor Jesus*. His body
exposed in each church, with blood splurged
from wounds so intense I can't look again.
  The pudgy mouth hooks in her nipple, hurts.
  She shivers, yet smiles at me smiling at them.

Crossing Borders, Pursued by the Feathered Serpent

In the train snaking the airport loop,
pinned to the seat by a robot's voice, I am alone.

I doze off and stare at the serpents devouring
skeletons. A frieze of eagles

eating human hearts. Cut in stone. Silent.
Then that man, Harry, in a hammock.

Jungle sounds. Anaconda's embrace.
Coils, wriggling limbs. The shriek.

The automaton at the gate chokes, spits out
my boarding pass, my name misspelled.

In the crammed Boeing: a snoring man with a wide open
mouth, ice cubes crushed into plastic glasses,

the rattle of opening cans.
I wobble on the edge of sound and silence.

The Train That Leaves

Remember the math problem about two trains
leaving at the same time from two cities, A and B,
coming toward each other at different speeds?

"Let's get on the train," Alice says to her friend,
"you at the main station in B, I at the station in A."
She starts the calculations.

It is precisely 10 o'clock; the train is about to pull away.

Alice rushes onto the platform. The big hand
moves slightly. She is late.

She takes off her high heels and runs,
holding tight her books, her purse and shoes.
People begin shouting warnings or advice.

The train has to leave so the school children
may begin their calculations.

Somebody tries to stop her, somebody stretches out
his arms, helps her into the carriage. The books spill
onto the platform, pages waving, words disappearing.

Alice thinks about the school, her blue math book,
and her friend she has not seen in weeks, months, years.

Snow Dust on Lilacs

I apologize for the long absence (she might be calling from a prison,
some undisclosed location; I am surprised by the thought). Working
odd jobs (a small chocolate shop, the blurry-eyed shift in a bakery–I run

through an old list) to make ends meet, she says, helping my family,
babysitting for my nephew (the one who was deployed in the Balkans,
fell in love with a Serb, I recall), my elderly relatives (ah, the almost-

blind uncle who didn't want to leave his aging house). Thank you for
leaving messages on my answering machine (her voice deep, reassuring,
like her recording). And I am late again with my Christmas cards

(by February I used to worry what the absence meant), she chuckles,
but I'll get to them. Yours mean a lot to me, I deeply appreciate your
keeping in touch (truly, all her cards are thoughtful, personalized–like

that Victorian girl smelling lilacs, and a bookmark). The ancient farmhouse
is charming (so, she is still renting–her furniture, her books in storage for
years). Creaking wood panels (I smell floor wax), crooked walls.

The photograph of lilacs you sent me hangs by the window looking out at
rows of cabbage, herbs–empty now but for threadbare patches of snow–
and flowers that I grow. Zinnias, poppies, cornflowers, you will love them,

she promises, when you come in late spring or summer. This year I will
call you for sure when I fly back from Florida (visiting her brother, I think).
Sorry, I didn't call last summer (or the ones before). Be patient with me.
Don't give up on me. I will call. I have to go now. Bye, bye.

What Are the Flowers Saying

Anna and I bring flowers. We arrange them one by one.
Purple-fluted poppies in a malachite vase. Round-faced
yellow zinnias in a wide-neck jar. Vibrant colors in each house.

Every day I tend to mine, add water, rearrange. Alstroemeria flames
of pink and orange slowly fade, open their coronas wide,
finally, hesitant, shed their tear-shaped petals.

When colors pale and leaves begin to wilt, blemishes appear,
Anna throws her flowers away. More than once
she has told me: I know there will be new ones.

Today she takes her husband to another specialist. In her living room
I see one Alstroemeria trimmed low, a lone survivor.
In the foyer, two magenta twigs saved from a large bouquet.

Where the Moonflowers Bloom

Still immersed in the blurry dream—
was the woman patting a horse, waving at me?

While pressing the computer's *on* switch
I detect a brown-shaped motion

at the wall of the house next-door,
where the white flowers open and close.

I grab my camera. *Movie* setting, I decide,
and film the deer sniffing the plant—is he raising

his bent leg to his head, waving at me?
The window rail and gauzy curtain pleats

impede the view, so I run out,
camera now set to *still photograph.*

He is there by the moon plant, immobile now,
velvety antlers boldly drawn against

the vinyl-siding strips. I press the shutter release
just once before he bolts for the hill's wilderness.

I head back to my house, load the chip
into the slot of the black box.

The scene replays in pixels. I save
him and the moonflowers, then click

my sister's name. I send them across the ocean
over the solid and ethereal impediments.

Notes

"The Thin Blue Line between Still and Alive"
Mazovian plain: Mazovia—a geographically and historically distinctive region in central Poland where, among others, Frederic Chopin was born and lived.

"Sunday Like No Other"
Martial law was declared in Poland by the Communist government on December 13, 1981. Solidarność: Independent Self-governing Trade Union "Solidarity," founded on September 17, 1980 at the Gdańsk Shipyard, with Lech Wałęsa as its leader—the first trade union in a Warsaw Pact country not controlled by the Communist Party.

"Fabled Roosters of Kazimierz"
Kazimierz Dolny: one of the most beautifully situated towns in Poland, on the eastern bank of the Vistula river; a painters' paradise; a historic monument (most prosperous in the 16th and early-17th centuries).

"Darkness of Her Head"
Poem inspired by Gauguin's painting *Mona Tupapau* in the Albright-Knox museum in Buffalo, New York. Tupapaus: Tahitian personifications of the spirits of death.

"In the Background the Waltz from *Doctor Zhivago*"
Katyń: the name of a forest in western Russia, near the city of Smolensk; one of the sites of, and also the metonym for, the mass executions of 22,000 Polish nationals by NKVD, the Soviet secret police, carried out in April and May 1940.

"The Voices"
Meja: a village near Gjakova/Đakovica in western Kosovo; and Prizren:

Prizren municipality in Kosovo, sites of massacres in the Kosovo War, 1998-1999. Columbine: Columbine High School shooting, April 20, 1999.

"An Artist Paints the Event"
A painting of the animals and the Ark by C. Foell, 1993 (as per my reading on the back of it) encountered at an art fair in Maryland.

"The Sun Comes Out in San Luis Potosí"
San Luis Potosí: the capital and most populous city in the Mexican state of San Luis Potosí. Churrigueresque: a lavishly exuberant Spanish baroque style characterized by elaborate surface decoration or its Latin-American adaptation.

"Echocardiogram"
Red River: April 1997 flooding of Grand Rapids, ND, by the Red River.

"This Is Not My Stomach"
After Magritte's line, beneath his unmistakable painting of a pipe: "Ceci n'est pas une pipe." (This is not a pipe.)

Acknowledgments

My heartfelt thanks go to Michael Salcman, the judge of this fifth edition of the Clarinda Harriss Poetry Prize contest, for his time and generosity, and to countless friends who have touched my life and my poems. Grateful acknowledgment is made to the following publications in which these poems appeared first, sometimes in a slightly different form:

"while trying to peel off," *Inner Art Journal*

"The Thin Blue Line between Still and Alive," *Spillway*

"My Mother at Twelve," *International Poetry Review* and in *Face Half-Illuminated* (Apprentice House, 2014)

"The Movie in My Head," *Little Patuxent Review*

"May Day," *Free State Review*

"Queuing for Lenin," *Beltway Poetry Quarterly*

"Sunday Like No Other," *The Potomac*

"At the Seaside Café," *Little Patuxent Review*

"Paintings in a Gray-Walled Waiting Room," *Off the Coast*

"Fabled Roosters of Kazimierz," *CITIES, A Book of Poems* (ed. S. Philip, Chuffed Buff Books, London, 2014)

"Luckie Shows Up Seventy Years Later," *Dogs Singing, A Tribute Anthology* (ed. Jessie Lendennie, Salmon Poetry Ltd., County Clare, Ireland, 2010)

"Visitation," *Pirene's Fountain*

"Darkness of Her Head," as "After Gauguin," *Theodate*

"Girl in the Red Coat," *A NARROW FELLOW Journal of Poetry*

"In the Background the Waltz from *Doctor Zhivago*," *International Poetry Review*

"The Voices," *Loch Raven Review*

"Echocardiogram" as " Echo—Testing My Heart," *Rufous Salon*

"An Artist Paints the Event," *The Baltimore Review*

"The Sun Comes Out in San Luis Potosí" as " San Luis Potosí:

Beginning," *Pivot*

"Crossing Borders, Pursued by the Feathered Serpent," *Driftwood Press*

"Snow Dust on Lilacs," *Kind of a Hurricane Press*

About the Poet

Danuta E. Kosk-Kosicka is the author of *Face Half-Illuminated*, a book of poems, translations, and prose (Apprentice House, 2014) and the translator for two bilingual books by Lidia Kosk, *niedosyt/ reshapings* and *Słodka woda, słona woda/Sweet Water, Salt Water*. Her poems, translations, essays, and interviews have appeared in the USA and throughout Europe in *Akcent; Driftwood Press; International Poetry Review; Lalitamba; Little Patuxent Review; Loch Raven Review; Notre Dame Review; Passager; Przegląd Polski, Nowy Dziennik; The Baltimore Review;* and elsewhere. A biochemist, bilingual poet and translator, photographer, and co-editor of *Loch Raven Review*, she grew up in Poland and lives in Maryland.

About CityLit Press

CityLit Press's mission is to provide a venue for writers who might otherwise be overlooked by larger publishers due to the literary nature or regional focus of their projects. It is the imprint of nonprofit CityLit Project, founded in Baltimore in 2004.

CityLit nurtures the culture of literature in Baltimore and throughout Maryland by creating enthusiasm for literature, building a community of avid readers and writers. Thank you to our major supporters: the National Endowment for the Arts, the Maryland State Arts Council, the Baltimore Office of Promotion and The Arts, and the Baltimore Community Foundation. More information and documentation is available at www.guidestar.org.

Additional support is provided by individual contributors. Financial support is vital for sustaining the ongoing work of the organization. Secure on-line donations can by made at our web site (click on "Donate").

CityLit is a member of the Greater Baltimore Cultural Alliance, the Maryland Association of Nonprofit Organizations, Maryland Citizens for the Arts, and the Writers' Conferences and Centers division of the Association of Writing Programs (AWP).

For submission guidelines, information about CityLit Press's poetry chapbook contest, and public programs offered by CityLit, please visit www.citylitproject.org.

ART WORKS.
arts.gov

MARYLAND STATE ARTS COUNCIL

BALTIMORE
OFFICE OF PROMOTION & THE ARTS

B C F
BALTIMORE
COMMUNITY
FOUNDATION

About the Harriss Poetry Prize

Launched in 2009 under the guidance of poet and CityLit Project chair Michael Salcman, the Harriss Poetry Prize is named in honor of Clarinda Harriss, eminent Baltimore poet, publisher, and professor of English at Towson University. Harriss, educated at Johns Hopkins University and Goucher College, is a widely published, award-winning poet and she serves as director of BrickHouse Books, Maryland's oldest literary press, which *Baltimore* magazine named "Best of Baltimore."

2014 Judge: Michael Salcman
2013 Judge: Marie Howe
2012 Judge: Tom Lux
2011 Judge: Dick Allen
2010 Judge: Michael Salcman

For complete guidelines, please go to www.citylitproject.org and click on "CityLit Press." Send entry fee, manuscript with table of contents, acknowledgments, and two coversheets (one with name, title, mailing address, daytime phone, and email address and one with title only) to:

Harriss Poetry Prize
CityLit Press
c/o CityLit Project
120 S. Curley Street
Baltimore, MD 21224

Annual submission deadline is December 1 (postmarked).

Previous Winners

Asphalt by Rebekah Remington
ISBN: 978-1936328-15-4
   "I love how Remington's mind moves from this
to that in some utterly lived syllogism ('What looks
like failure is something else'). I love how the poet—
desperate as the rest of us—loves the world."
                                          Marie Howe, Judge

Every Bit of It by Katherine Bogden
ISBN: 978-1936328-08-6
   "This book reveals by what it hides. It tells a deeply
human story and tells it slant, as Emily Dickinson
said, when, I believe, she was talking about how
originality might come about. And that's what these
poems are: original. And alive."
                                          Tom Lux, Judge

Famous by Bruce Sager
ISBN: 978-1936328-06-2
   "Only twice before, in the many times I've judged
poetry contests, has a poet's work stood out as
strongly as Sager's."
                                          Dick Allen, Judge

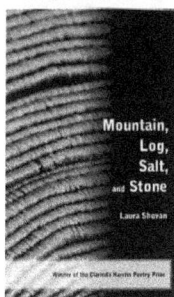

Mountain, Log, Salt, and Stone by Laura Shovan
ISBN: 978-1936328-02-4
   "Laura Shovan enlivens her quotidian subjects
with a shrewd and powerful use of metaphor,
a critical strategy all too often neglected in
contemporary work."
                                          Michael Salcman, Judge

www.ingramcontent.com/pod-product-compliance
Lightning Source LLC
Chambersburg PA
CBHW031540040426
42445CB00010B/626